WIN
YOUR DAY,
WIN
YOUR LIFE

THIRTY AFFIRMATIONS TO
UNLOCK YOUR GREATER

DARRELL A. PALMES, III

DEDICATION

To everyone who desires greater...

CONTENTS

Week 4: FINANCES

BONUS: FUN

INTRODUCTION

I first heard of the Five F's (Faith, Family, Fitness, Finances and Fun) in two thousand and seven on the Yolanda Adams Morning Show while driving in Atlanta. A few months later in January two thousand and eight, God revealed to me that He wanted me to become a pastor. I speak more in-depth about this encounter in my first book, "Called To Something Greater," so I won't share all of those details again. However, I remember saying to God that if I was going to do this thing called pastoral ministry, I didn't want to be known only as a preacher. Because of various situations and struggles I had faced in life, I wanted my ministry to bring total healing to people — not just spiritual.

In addition to those who were seeking to develop a closer relationship with God, I needed to speak life to those like me who had interesting family dynamics. I know what it's like to lose a parent. I know what it's like to struggle to find your identity in a blended family. I know what it's like to be kicked out of the house. I also know what it's like to voluntarily leave home as a teenager and become completely homeless, all because you aren't happy with the family dynamics.

I needed to speak life to people who struggle with their

appearance (including weight and shape) and overall physical and emotional health. In addition to always being sad due to my family challenges, I was constantly teased for being the fat kid growing up. Plus I was ashy — the type of ashy that even cocoa butter had a hard time hiding. Being sad and being teased caused me to turn to destructive habits. It wasn't until I became a teenager and started playing football in high school that I began to work out; not because I was focused on my health, but so I could avoid being teased. Admittedly, a piece of me focuses on my health the way I currently do because I don't want to be talked about as the fat guy in the room.

In the late nineties, I became interested in computers and technology. I decided to enter the information technology (IT) field and eventually consulted for various companies and governmental agencies like Dell, the Centers for Disease Control and Prevention (CDC), multiple HBCUs, and, most recently, Emory University. God allowed me to be skilled in IT, so my ministry allowed me to teach people how to have a successful career in the tech industry while earning great money in the process.

I absolutely love to travel, and cruises are my favorite way to vacation! Not only can I enjoy what the ship has to offer; I get to enjoy the various beaches and destinations along the way. Being able to experience multiple cultures within the same week fascinates me. I also enjoy seeing my family enjoying themselves. Whether that be traveling together, going on a family walk, sitting on the couch watching a movie, going to look at Christmas lights during the holiday season or everything else in between...seeing them happy makes me happy. We work too hard not to have fun. And there is no better way to experience fun than with those you love.

When I began to reflect on the things that mattered most to me and the things I wanted to focus on in my ministry, God reminded me of what I'd heard on the radio in two thousand and seven. So, in January of two thousand and eight, after saying yes to the call on my life, I created a personal mission statement for myself: "Helping people have greater faith, family, fitness, finances and fun."

In this book you'll read about strategies to assist you in each of those areas of your life. Just like LeBron James, Dwyane Wade and Chris Bosh joined forces in Miami as the "Big Three" and went on to win multiple championships together, I pray that you look at these areas as the "Big Five." To win the championship of life, all five components must work together. If you already have a good relationship with God, work on your family. If you already have a good relationship with your family, work on leaving an inheritance to your children's children. If your finances are on point but you're spending all of your money on medical bills because of your poor eating choices and lack of exercise and proper rest, make whatever adjustments you need to make to arrive at optimal health.

I've designed this book to take your life from good to greater in thirty days. Greater is possible for you, if you simply apply the information. While I appreciate you supporting the movement with this purchase, I'd much rather you be part of the movement with your lifestyle.

I'll either see you at the top or from the top. Your daily choices will determine from where you're seen. So let's go...it's time to unlock your greater!

WEEK ONE
FAITH

"To one who has faith, no explanation is necessary. To one without faith, no explanation is possible."

- Thomas Aquinas

AFFIRMATION 1:

FAITH THAT I AM SAVED!

*"God saved you by His grace when you believed.
And you can't take credit for this; it is a gift from God."
– Ephesians 2:8*

When thinking about how to deliver the most impact and value to your life through this book, I was faced with an interesting dilemma: Should I begin this devotional by discussing finances? After all, many people equate greatness with the size of their bank account or their salaries. So, I considered getting straight to the point with a bold, attention-grabbing statement such as "God is getting ready to blow your mind in this new season! Declare and decree right now that you are a millionaire!" I'm certain, no matter who you are, that such a declaration would make you want to keep reading.

Undoubtedly, there's truth to most of those statements. However, I concluded that the only way in good conscience I could help you begin your journey to winning your day — and ultimately and more importantly your life — is by reminding you of your need for salvation. If you're not a Christian or don't believe in God at all, that's OK. Keep reading, as you may find the principles in this book extremely helpful to you as you pursue greater. Now, you may be asking what salvation has to do with faith. Great question!

The first step to being saved is to want to be saved and to ask Christ to come into your life as your Lord and Savior. Believe that He can change your life and make you whole, then confess with your mouth and believe (there's that word again) with your heart that Jesus Christ is your Lord and Savior. If you truly desire to experience salvation, say this with me: "Lord, please forgive me of my sins. I declare that from this day forward, You will be the Lord of my life." That's it! That's the prayer.

And if you prayed that prayer, congratulations because you just got saved! My sincere apologies if you were expecting me to say something deeply profound and theological about the process of salvation; however, the reality is your salvation was instantaneous the moment you prayed that prayer. And one of the things I love about salvation is you don't have to look a certain way, live in a certain neighborhood or belong to a certain church. Salvation is a free gift to all who accept it.

Now that your salvation is secure, I'd like to help you put in the work to secure your destiny. But let me caution you that securing your destiny won't be as easy as obtaining your salvation. Because you've chosen to be saved, you'll find that there are many "temptations" that will try to derail you, many temptations to try to lure you from your walk with Christ and your overall pursuit of greater. However, if you apply the tools in the rest of this book, I assure you that the rest of your life, will be the best of your life. So...here's to your future!

#WinYourDay Affirmation:

Today, I will make the decision to make
Jesus Christ Lord of my life.

REFLECTIONS

_____

_____

_____

_____

_____

_____

_____

_____

_____

_____

_____

_____

_____

_____

_____

_____

_____

_____

AFFIRMATION 2:

FAITH THROUGH HEARING

"So then faith cometh by hearing,
and hearing by the word of God."
- Romans 10:17 KJV

We used two words interchangeably yesterday: faith and believe. So how does one have faith or belief in something? Today's scripture tells us faith comes by hearing. But hearing what, exactly? That's easy. The answer is hearing the word of The Lord. We typically listen to a lot of things, including music, social media, our relatives and friends. But if you truly want to level up in life, you're going to have to start listening to the word of God. God speaks to us in a variety of ways, and the method I find to be most effective is the Bible. But I can't just read for reading's sake. In other words, I have to actually believe what the Bible says about me. That's right. When the Word says I am more than a conqueror, I have to believe it for it to be so. When it says I am the head and not the tail, the lender and not the borrower, I have to believe it! Blessed? I believe it; therefore, I am!

One of the main ways to your "greater" is through your belief system. And the best way to boost your belief system is to flood your mind with the promises in God's word. Read it. Believe it. Speak it. (We'll talk about speaking later.) Think of it like taking a test. You can't perform well on a test if you don't know the material that will be covered on it. Likewise, you can't know the promises God speaks over you/your life if you don't read — and study — His word.

#WinYourDay Affirmation:
Today I will spend time in God's Word, the Bible, and ask Him to help me believe every promise He has spoken over my life.

REFLECTIONS

_____
_____
_____
_____
_____
_____
_____
_____
_____
_____
_____
_____
_____
_____
_____
_____
_____
_____

AFFIRMATION 3:

FAITH THROUGH SEEING

"Faith shows the reality of what we hope for;
it is the evidence of things we cannot see."
- Hebrews 11:1

If you truly want to win your life, you must learn to see it before you see it. I'm not talking about sight. I'm talking vision. Vision shows you what's possible in life, while sight shows what you have — and what you're lacking — at the time. So many of you get caught up in your present conditions: your marriage is shaky, the bank account is low, you're overweight and unfit, the house is too small, etc. While it's natural to see what you have, to achieve greater, you must see what you want. 2 Corinthians 5:7 (that's Second Corinthians, by the way) says, "For we walk by faith and not by sight." Don't worry about where you are; have a vision for where you're going.

Visualize your relationship with God. Visualize a happy and blessed marriage. Visualize experiencing joy with your children — whether biological or adopted — around the dinner table. Visualize your ideal body weight and shape. Visualize that dream house, job, car and vacation. And if you're having a tough time seeing yourself in the future, remember what God says about you: You are blessed, you are chosen, you are loved, you are saved, you are victorious, you are wealthy, your relationships are blessed and you are more than a conqueror! Think of everything that awaits you, all of the blessings God promises, as a five-course meal. But remember, you can't order from the menu without first visualizing what you need/want.

#WinYourDay Affirmation:

Today, I will not be blinded by my present situation, and I will visualize all of the things I want to achieve.

REFLECTIONS

AFFIRMATION 4:

FAITH THROUGH SPEAKING

"You don't have enough faith," Jesus told them. "I tell you the truth, if you had faith even as small as a mustard seed, you could say to this mountain, 'Move from here to there,' and it would move. Nothing would be impossible."
- Matthew 17:20

Have you heard the phrase, "You're doing too much?" Or what about, "It doesn't take all of that!?" Well, as it relates to faith, these two phrases couldn't be more accurate. Today's text, which tells us that a small amount of faith can move mountains, contains two important parts. First, it doesn't take all of that! In other words, you don't have to have a large amount of faith to get big results in your life. Some people have big faith — or mad faith as the younger crowd might say. That's cool. But everyone doesn't have it like that. And trust me, if you don't possess unquestionable faith, I can relate. At times things happen in life that cause our faith to wane. But it's all good. Why? Because the text reminds us that a little can go a long way when used correctly. In a way it's like the adage, "Less is more." Jesus isn't requiring us to have enormous faith, enough to fill a 100,000-seat football stadium. He's asking us to have at least a little faith. Of course, the more faith you have, and the more you witness Christ supplying your needs, your faith will likely increase.

Second, with a small amount of faith you can speak to giant obstacles and command them to move from your path. Never, and I mean NEVER underestimate the importance of your words. Genesis 1:3 says, "And God said, 'Let there be light,' and there was light." God literally created the entire world with His voice. It wasn't until the sixth day of creation that God used His hands to create — something we'll talk about later. Since God said it, and you and I were created in the image of God, we can accomplish things by speaking them, too! And when we speak, the universe has to respond to our voices. So be careful of the words you speak, because they have the power to either create worlds or destroy them. (Proverbs 18:21) Speak wisely!

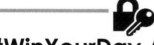

#WinYourDay Affirmation:
Today, I will tell my health, my marriage, my friendships, my relationships with coworkers, my finances and every other area of my life, LET THERE BE LIGHT!

REFLECTIONS

_____

_____

_____

_____

_____

_____

_____

_____

_____

_____

_____

_____

_____

_____

_____

_____

_____

_____

AFFIRMATION 5:

FAITH THROUGH WRITING

*"And the Lord answered me, and said, Write the vision,
and make it plain upon tables..."*
- Habakkuk 2:2

It's very difficult, if not impossible, to hit a target you can't see. To achieve greater, you need to write down what you visualize. The problem most people have is their dreams, goals and aspirations are in their head and when it's time to execute them, they don't know where to begin. Before I understood this concept, I had a lot of ideas but often grew frustrated over my lack of progress with them — which stemmed from operating from memory instead of on paper.

Neuroscience suggests that we are one hundred twenty percent to one hundred forty percent more likely to remember what is written down than what we think in our heads. Our text today reminds us to plainly write down the vision — what we've believed, heard, seen and said — so that when others see it they can run with it. In other words, you'll have a greater chance of success at reaching your goals when you write them down and look at them regularly.

Looking at them regularly can be easy, especially if you place them in areas you frequent daily like the refrigerator door, the bathroom door or even the front door if you're one of the people who's still working outside the home. Write down your goals and have them staring you in the face. For that matter, the bathroom mirror is another good place to put them. The more you see your goals, my hope is that you will develop an even stronger desire to do what you must to ensure they come to fruition.

Make no mistake: writing brings clarity, and clarity results in focus.

#WinYourDay Affirmation:

Today, I will write down the vision God has declared over my life. I will also write down every dream, goal and idea that I want to accomplish.

REFLECTIONS

_____

_____

_____

_____

_____

_____

_____

_____

_____

_____

_____

_____

_____

_____

_____

_____

AFFIRMATION 6:

FAITH THROUGH RUNNING

"So that a runner can carry the correct message to others."
- Habakkuk 2:2

Let's get down to the nitty gritty. At some point, you're going to have to stop visualizing the same goals and writing down the same concepts and just get to work! Yes, you have to hear it, see it, say it and write it. But eventually, you're going to have to run it! You can't lose weight without putting in the work. Whether that means eating healthier than you're accustomed to or exercising more than you'd like; eventually you must put in the work to get your desired results.

I hate to say it, but the check isn't coming in the mail — unless you put in the work. Your relationship isn't going to get better by osmosis or just because you want it to. You're not going to pass the class unless you show up for class and pay attention! And most of us are way too old to wish upon a star! So just get to work already because the success of your greater depends heavily on your work ethic. If you don't know where to begin, start with your favorite Internet search engine, then get off the 'Net and apply what you've learned! Don't make the mistake that was referenced in Proverbs 21:25, "Despite their desires, the lazy will come to ruin, for their hands refuse to work."

Nowadays, it seems a lot of people want a lot of nice things but they just don't want to put in the work to have those nice things. Let me be the first to tell you that a hard day's work never hurt anybody. And if you know what I know, sometimes you have to put in overtime or even double-time. And let's not forget about part-time. A part-time hustle might be what's needed in order to fulfill your full-time dreams. Talk to most people in their forties and up and I'm sure you'll learn that many of them have worked a part-time job and a full-time job at some point in their lives. It's called doing what you have to do to get the things you want to have. It's fine to have faith that you're going to achieve a certain status — or reach certain goals — in life. But remember, James 2:14 says it best: Faith without works is dead.

#WinYourDay Affirmation:
Today I will complete one action item on my list of goals and dreams. If God is for me, who can be against me?!

REFLECTIONS

_____

_____

_____

_____

_____

_____

_____

_____

_____

_____

_____

_____

_____

_____

_____

_____

_____

AFFIRMATION 7:

FAITH THROUGH WAITING

"For the vision is yet for an appointed time, but at the end it shall speak, and not lie: though it tarry, wait for it; because it will surely come, it will not tarry."
– Habakkuk 2:3

Listen, friends. Shy of hitting the lottery or inheriting a large sum of money or property, it's very difficult to get wealthy overnight. Likewise, you're not going to lose thirty pounds overnight. Your relationship won't go from barely surviving to thriving overnight. And your bad habit(s) or addiction(s) won't be broken overnight.

Let's be realistic. You didn't get in this position of need overnight, so you shouldn't expect to be on the other side of it so quickly.

Think about it. If success came quickly, virtually everyone would be successful! True greater (in God and on earth) comes from being consistent to the vision. The text says, "...though the vision is taking a while, wait for it, because it's going to come to pass!" Simply put, no one can sow and reap in the same season. The same year? Yes! The same season? No. The key is to just keep grinding. Keep growing. Keep showing up. Keep loving on your spouse.

Keep putting in the work because eventually you'll reap what you've sown.

Any gardener will tell you that if you put good in, you'll get either the same good out or more of it! Likewise, if you put bad in, you'll get the same bad out — or more of it! Choose what you sow wisely. And if you realize the seeds you're sowing aren't prospering or enhancing your life in significant ways, perhaps it's time to start sowing different seeds. Have you ever heard someone say, "it's like throwing good money after bad?" Well, don't keep going in the same direction if you know it's not leading to a path of success. If you're exercising to lose weight but you're not dropping any pounds, maybe you need to consider doing different exercises. Or, maybe you need to include a better diet and proper sleep/rest with your exercises. If you want your relationship to get better, do things to strengthen it and stop doing things that are weakening it or causing friction. I could go on and on, but by now I hope you get the point: Success isn't going to simply happen. <u>Instead, you must put in the work to make it happen!</u>

#WinYourDay Affirmation:
Today, I will plant good seeds and wait patiently for the harvest to arrive.

REFLECTIONS

_____

_____

_____

_____

_____

_____

_____

_____

_____

_____

_____

_____

_____

_____

_____

_____

_____

_____

WEEK TWO
FAMILY

"What can you do to promote world peace?
Go home and love your family."

- Mother Theresa

AFFIRMATION 8:

GREATER SINGLES

"Then the Lord God formed the man from the dust of the ground. He breathed the breath of life into the man's nostrils, and the man became a living person."
- Genesis 2:7

According to the account of creation found in the Bible, The Lord created everything on days one through five by voice command. On the sixth day, instead of speaking He knelt down and formed man out of the dust of the earth. (This proves there are some aspects to your "greater" that you can't simply speak into existence. Instead, you're going to have to dirty your hands and get to work!)

While Adam and Eve were created on the same day, there was a period of time when only Adam and His Creator were in relationship with each other. If you're single and really want to get to the next level in your life, whether that's obtaining a promotion on your job, purchasing your first home, landing your dream job or even getting married, you're going to have to first develop a relationship with the Lord, your Creator. Before Adam obtained all of the material things — including his job naming the animals — it was just him and God. Adam became a homeowner after he developed a relationship with God. Likewise, Adam got boo'd up with

Eve, his forever girl, after his relationship with God was established. (Incidentally, fellas, please stop asking your wife to take care of everything in the house. After all, it was your house and you had to handle things before she became a part of your world, so don't try to dump all of the household responsibilities on her once you two become one.)

Take your gift of singleness and use the time to discover who God is to you. Also, embrace the opportunity to become the best person you can be at this stage of your life. By already having a relationship with God, Adam was "husband material" before Eve came along. Likewise, ladies, you should focus on becoming "wife material" before your Adam arrives. Now, I get it that it's not good for anyone to be alone, and we all have a need for human interaction, contact and relationships. The need for connectivity is ingrained in our DNA. However, don't let your desire for connectivity cause you to make decisions and connections (you know the ones) that you'll later regret.

So, here it is in short: "If you seek God first and His righteousness, EVERYTHING else will be added unto you." Matthew 6:33.

#WinYourDay Affirmation:
Today I will get to know God in a personal way like Adam did.

REFLECTIONS

AFFIRMATION 9:

GREATER HUSBANDS

"For husbands, this means love your wives,
just as Christ loved the church..."
- Ephesians 5:25

More than anything else, your wife needs and wants your love. The same way you want and desire the physical side of love; she wants and needs the emotional side of love. A great resource for you is "The Five Love Languages," a nineteen ninety-two book by Gary Chapman that outlines five ways couples express and experience love: quality time, acts of service, gift-giving, physical touch and words of affirmation.

To express love through quality time, consider establishing a "Date Night" with your wife each week. It doesn't have to be expensive. In fact, you can stay home and have a perfect date night by snuggling on the couch while watching a movie, dusting off the vinyl (vinyl was before we streamed music by the way) and dancing to music from back in the day or cooking your favorite meal together. Of course if you want to go out, that's cool, too. Just do what is necessary to invest in quality time together.

If your wife wants to experience love through physical

touch, don't just get right to it, fellas! Hug her, kiss her, hold her hand — and don't expect sex in return. Now if it happens, hallelujah! No matter what, please be aware that physical touch is MUCH MORE than sex. For example, one of the most endearing ways you can kiss a woman is gently on the forehead. And you may not think it's sexy, but massaging a woman's temples and/or her feet is a sure-fire way to make her feel the love.

If she prefers gifts, flowers, cards and jewelry (if you're into jewelry) are always safe bets, but go that extra mile when you can. If you've noticed her expressing interest in something being sold on an informercial, surprise her with it. Or, if she loves to read but doesn't have time between work, the kids, grocery shopping, etc., buy her some audiobooks that she can listen to in the car or while soaking in the tub. No matter what you buy her, fellas, don't give her gifts only on her birthday, your wedding anniversary, Valentine's Day or Christmas. Every now and then, buy her something "just because."

Now if your wife likes to be motivated, tell her often that you appreciate the way she handles her business and that she's a good friend, mother, wife, etc. Don't just give random words of affirmation but instead make your words count.

Finally, if she receives love through acts of service, then tonight I want you to wash, dry and put up the dishes. Or cook dinner. And again, do so without expecting sex in return.

Men, if on a daily basis you love your wife the way she

needs and wants to be loved, the rest of your marriage will be the best of your marriage!

#WinYourDay Affirmation:
Today, I will tell my wife I love her and will show her by my actions.

REFLECTIONS

_____

_____

_____

_____

_____

_____

_____

_____

_____

_____

_____

_____

_____

_____

_____

_____

_____

_____

AFFIRMATION 10:

GREATER WIVES

"...the wife must respect her husband."
- Ephesians 5:33

Ladies, while you need and want love, your husband needs and wants respect. Just as your heart desires affection, his heart craves respect. I've seen too many relationships break up because while the wife loves her husband, she doesn't respect him — or at least her actions signal to him that she doesn't. Respect the decisions he makes in the marriage. Now, I'm not saying he should make all of the decisions by himself. After all, ladies, you have value and your voices needs to be heard, too. But by the same token, if there's a stalemate and a decision must be made, give him room to make the final decision. If his decision ends up being wrong, don't say, "I told you so!" Instead, let him know you still love him and y'all will find a way to get through it together. (Of course, if he repeatedly makes the wrong call, you may want to discuss allowing you to make the final decisions for a while as he re-evaluates his decisions and where he went wrong.)

This is just one example of how to respect your husband. Others include, but aren't limited to, communicating with him without being brash and abrasive, focusing on what he does well instead of harping only on what he does wrong, acknowledging his leadership and telling him you appreciate him — all of which may prevent him from being passive.

From an early age when we're but boys, we are taught that we are supposed to be "the man of the house." We're taught to be the providers and the ones who make the decisions. I realize we're in the twenty-first century and things have changed. Likewise, I realize in many relationships the woman — not the man — is the breadwinner. I get it. Even so, ladies, remember that if a man isn't made to feel like a man, if things are said and/or done that emasculate him, that likely will cause him to harbor resentment toward you. He'll end up having issues with you and with himself, issues that certainly won't translate into him loving you. Just remember, ladies, without feeling confident that he has your respect, it will be difficult for him to give you his love.

#WinYourDay Affirmation:
Today, I will tell and show my husband that I respect him as my husband and also as the man of the house.

REFLECTIONS

_____

_____

_____

_____

_____

_____

_____

_____

_____

_____

_____

_____

_____

_____

_____

_____

_____

_____

AFFIRMATION 11:

GREATER KIDS

"Honor your father and mother. Then you will live a long, full life in the land the Lord your God is giving you."
- Exodus 20:12

Honor is so important to accessing your greater. All of us are children and need to learn how to honor the people God put in our lives to help mold and shape us into who we are today. Honor gives us access to longevity. For centuries there's been talk of a so-called fountain of youth. Want to live a long life? Honor your mother and father and you may live a long life.

What if you had a bad relationship with your parents? You should still honor them. The command doesn't say honor your parents if they treated you right. It just says honor. If the relationship with your parents is less than ideal, this might be tough to do. However, honoring your parents despite the relationship is where the real blessing comes in. And if you've lost your parents, find a way to honor their memory by being the best person you can be. You can also honor those who helped raise you, including pastors, coaches, teachers, legal guardians, etc.

Honoring your parents can mean more than obeying them. You honor your parents by doing well in school — if you're of school age — or by doing well on your job if you're a young adult who's working. You honor your parents by being respectful of elders and by being known as a nice young man or young woman. You honor your parents by not doing things to bring shame to them or to the family name. You honor your parents by not forgetting the valuable lessons they taught you when you were younger. And you honor your parents by instilling those valuable lessons in your own children — if or when you have them — or in your nieces and nephews or children in your church or neighborhood. Check out dictionary.com and under the word honor — some twenty-three definitions in — it says "to show respect to and to be a credit to." Remember, you honor your parents in many ways — not just in "obeying them."

#WinYourDay Affirmation:

Today, I will show honor to my parents and those who were a part of the village that helped raise me.

REFLECTIONS

AFFIRMATION 12:

GREATER BLENDED FAMILIES

"But those who won't care for their relatives, especially those in their own household, have denied the true faith. Such people are worse than unbelievers."
- 1 Timothy 5:8

It is said that a child will always know the sound and scent of his or her mother because he or she knows her from the inside out. My birth mother died when I was fourteen-months-old. Unfortunately, I have no recollection of my mother's voice or scent because there were no recordings or items of hers that I could access. Suffice it to say, most of the trouble I got into as a child — and even as an adult if I'm honest — can be attributed to my longing to know my mother's voice. Even though I have an older biological sister, and even though my father remarried and I was blessed with a "bonus mother" and brother, losing my natural mother left me feeling alone and abandoned most of the time. I lacked a sense of belonging, which really intensified after my father and first bonus mother divorced. During that divorce, I went to live with my father, and my sister and brother went to live with my bonus mom. I wasn't even ten, and I'd already lost two moms — in addition to my older brother and sister. My father has had multiple marriages, and each marriage has brought a new bonus mother and siblings.

When I got married, I instantly became a bonus dad as my wife had a daughter from her previous marriage. Why am I telling you this? Because I know quite a bit about blended families and want to see your blended family succeed. Follow these four strategies and chances are it will.

First, never use words like step or adopted. Reference children only as "my kids." During a divorce or when parents split, children are already experiencing a shaky sense of belonging. Calling them your children or your kids versus using the words step or adopted can make them feel as though they're part of the family, instead of making them feel less-than. Children, on the other hand, should refer to their bonus dad or mom as their dad or mom — unless that causes friction with their biological parents. In that case, children should find nicknames that work for everyone. For example, Vice President Kamala Harris has two "bonus children" from her marriage to Doug Emhoff, who was married previously. Doug's children call the Vice President "Mamala," a blend of the words mom and Kamala. Children should always show respect to their bonus parents and not use terms such as stepmother or stepfather. Remember, you walk up and down steps — not each other.

Second, parents should always present a united front and NEVER say things like, "this is my child, not yours." Likewise, both parents should be able to discipline the children — despite whose children they are biologically speaking. And they should always remember that their spouse is the man or woman of the house and never allow their child or children to disrespect them. (I'd be remiss if I didn't mention there's a huge difference between discipline and abuse. If you or your spouse don't know the difference, don't be afraid to leave. I'm not an advocate for divorce, but I'm also not an advocate for domestic violence and/or child abuse.)

Third, if there are biological children as well as bonus children involved, parent all children the same way and spend the same amount of time with them — when humanly possible — to avoid the appearance of favoritism. I said when humanly possible because some children are more needy than others, are involved in more extra-curricular activities than others or could be special needs children and require more of your time.

Fourth, see a licensed family therapist once a quarter (more frequently if necessary) to ensure your blended family gets off to a great start and stays there! After all, when your marriage and family win, everything else in life is more enjoyable.

#WinYourDay Affirmation:
Today, I will follow these strategies to ensure my blended family is the best family in the neighborhood!

REFLECTIONS

AFFIRMATION 13:

GREATER TRAINING

"Train up a child in the way he should go..."
– Proverbs 22:6

I remember growing up and having daily family worship. My parents would wake my siblings and me up around six-thirty, Monday through Friday, to spend time praying and worshipping together. Sometimes I liked it as a child; sometimes I didn't. I mean, what kid wants to wake up that early in the morning anyway? But I can honestly say I've always remembered those worship gatherings. No matter what trouble I got into as a teenager, or even as an adult for that matter, I always remembered my father telling me the importance of putting God first in my life. And now that I'm not getting in as much trouble, LOL, and now that I have a family of my own, I strive to have worship in my household every single day. The text says if you train up a child in the way they should go, when he or she is older, he or she won't depart from it. This doesn't guarantee that just because you train your children in good ways they'll always be good. Instead it means the likelihood of their success as adults skyrockets because they've been instilled with good values.

Train your children to spend time with God every day.

Train your children to be loving and kind. However, don't just do this in word; also do this in deed. Your children are watching every move you make and listening to every word you say. If you want to give them the best chance of a successful life, make sure your actions and words match. Remember, it's children's nature, as well as their nurture, that make them who they are.

From the time children are born, they spend their early years watching their parents or guardians interact with society. When children are learning how to talk, they not only hear your words but literally watch your mouth to see how you're forming them. It also goes without saying that your children will repeat what you say and do what you do.

Let me also speak to those of you who don't have, or maybe can't have, children. Every child deserves a village. Just because you don't have biological children doesn't mean you can't still be a blessing to children. There are literally thousands of children that are waiting to be fostered and/or adopted, and you might be the answer to a child's prayer right now. If you aren't interested in becoming a child's legal guardian, consider becoming a mentor. There is a child waiting to receive instructions on how to become a better person, and you could have what he or she is looking for. Even if all you do is tell a young person how to avoid the mistakes you made at his or her age, that could go a long way. I beg you not to let the fact that you don't have children of your own stop you from blessing a child—now.

#WinYourDay Affirmation:

Today, I will train my kids to be the best little humans they can be so when they're bigger humans they will bring honor (see yesterday) to not only my family's name, but to The Lord's name as well.

REFLECTIONS

_____

_____

_____

_____

_____

_____

_____

_____

_____

_____

_____

_____

_____

_____

_____

_____

_____

AFFIRMATION 14:

GREATER FAMILIES

"...But as for me and my family, we will serve the Lord."
– Joshua 24:15

When Joshua made this declaration, he was surrounded by a generation of people who didn't want to follow The Lord's ways. Much like today, we are surrounded by a generation of people who no longer operate under their parents' or grandparents' religion. I'm not trying to cast shade on any family's view of God, but I think we can all agree that many families don't put God first. If you believe in God, it doesn't matter if you're a single-parent family, a traditional family or it's just you by yourself, it's your responsibility to make sure that every activity taking place in your home brings honor and glory to God. This doesn't just apply to your home or your apartment; it applies to your heart and mind as well.

Joshua made a declaration that no matter what chaos others were involved in or what foolishness they were doing, he and his house would go all the way with The Lord. They were going to do things God's way. If you truly want to achieve greater in this life, you're going to have to make the decision to do things God's way. You're going to have to serve Him with your life. Serve Him with your actions. Serve Him with your attitude.

Serve Him with your gifts, skills, talents and abilities. As one songwriter once said, "It takes your everything to serve The Lord."

#WinYourDay Affirmation:
Today, I will declare with my mouth and with my actions that I will serve The Lord with everything I have. And I will make sure those who live with me do the same.

REFLECTIONS

_____

_____

_____

_____

_____

_____

_____

_____

_____

_____

_____

_____

_____

_____

_____

_____

WEEK THREE
FITNESS

"It is health that is the real wealth, and not pieces of gold and silver."

- Mahatma Gandhi

AFFIRMATION 15:

GREATER WORDS

"The tongue can bring death or life; those who love to talk
will reap the consequences."
- Proverbs 18:21

I have a simple "health-related" question: Do you want to live or do you want to die? You see, before we can deal with your physical weight, we need to deal with your spiritual weight. Where you are in life directly correlates to the words you speak. The scripture says death and life come from our mouths — are in the power of the tongue. It goes on to say we will eat the fruits of whichever one we speak. You know it's funny how people like to take that scripture and flip the words to say life and death are in the power of the tongue. But if you read the scripture carefully, it says death before it says life. I believe the scripture's author coined it that way because we humans have a bad tendency of wanting to speak negativity over our lives before speaking positively. In other words, we speak death before we speak life.

Instead of commenting on what you don't have, comment and focus on what you do have. Give thanks for the money that's currently in your bank account. Give thanks for the state of your relationship. Give thanks for your present life. Even if your life isn't where you want it to be, you are alive to change it! Therefore, speak life by saying thank you, Lord, for a relationship that I can change through my actions. Speak life by saying thank you, Lord, for a bank account that will no longer barely have enough for a gallon of gas but will one day make me the one lending money versus borrowing it. Speak life over your physical health by saying even though the numbers on the scale aren't good, at least I'm alive to change the things I eat and drink and to change how often I exercise. Remember what I said earlier in this book: If you speak it, the universe has to respond. So, the first principle to managing your health both spiritually and physically is to watch your mouth.

#WinYourDay Affirmation:
Today, I will speak life over every aspect of my life, so that I can enjoy its fruit.

REFLECTIONS

_____

_____

_____

_____

_____

_____

_____

_____

_____

_____

_____

_____

_____

_____

_____

AFFIRMATION 16:

GREATER HEALTH

"So whether you eat or drink, or whatever you do,
do it all for the glory of God."
- 1 Corinthians 10:31

If you remember nothing else from this book, remember this: Every area of your life can prosper, but if your health is bad, it will impact how you enjoy the prosperous areas of your life. Your marriage can be phenomenal, but let's face it: Nobody wants to be around somebody who's breathing hard all of the time because of weight issues or other health challenges. You can be successful financially, but what difference does it make if you're spending all of your wealth on medical bills and medication for illnesses that in many cases can be avoided — like type two diabetes. Go ahead and blast me for that last statement if you want. But just know I come from a family of diabetics, and at one point I was diagnosed as pre-diabetic. I have witnessed how diabetes wreaked havoc on some of my family members, causing amputations and even death, while other family members made necessary diet and exercise changes to completely reverse the course. And I'm not just talking about diabetes here. I'm talking about addictions to nicotine, narcotics and/or alcohol, where you celebrate every win or loss in your life with a fifth of Hen or another drink of choice.

Simply put, it doesn't matter what you achieve in life if you're not healthy enough — or no longer alive — to enjoy your success. So make a decision right here and right now that you're going to concentrate on living a healthier lifestyle. If the COVID-19 pandemic has taught us anything, it's taught us that we never know what's coming and, that said, it's best to be in the best health possible. The number of Americans who have died from the coronavirus are heartbreaking and devastating, and it's no secret that some of the people who have succumbed to the illness very likely wouldn't have had it not been for underlying conditions. (Particularly among people of color.) Please know I'm not sitting in judgment of you and that I – like you – am a work in progress. But please also know we should always be cognizant of areas in which we need to do better.

#WinYourDay Affirmation:
Today, I will do everything in power to make sure I'm alive to enjoy all of the blessings God has for me.

REFLECTIONS

_____

_____

_____

_____

_____

_____

_____

_____

_____

_____

_____

_____

_____

_____

_____

_____

AFFIRMATION 17:

GREATER MENTAL HEALTH

"Beloved, I wish above all things that thou mayest prosper and be in health, even as thy soul prospereth."
– 3 John 1:2

There's nothing like being depressed. Trust me. I know. Depression can cause you to lose your appetite for food and drink and even make you think about taking your own life. There was a time when things had gotten so bad in my life that I thought about ending it all. But at the very moment I was going to do it, God gave me a glimpse of my son and how he needed a father in his life. A father that would show him how to be a Black man in today's world. A father that would show him how not to quit. A father that would show him it is possible to turn your mistakes into a ministry. A father that would show him how to be a good husband and father one day.

Through that glimmer of hope, God allowed me to connect with a mental health professional, as well as a brotherhood (shout out to the prayer line), that would keep me accountable in all areas of my life. I am going to make a statement as clearly as possible — and in all caps — to ensure you don't miss the point. FIND

A THERAPIST AND LIFE COACH TO HELP YOU NAVIGATE LIFE. The therapist will help you unpack your past, while the life coach will help you prepare for your future. Both are needed if you truly want to be in the best position to handle your greater. Make sure you are prosperous in your mind, body and soul.

#WinYourDay Affirmation:
Today, I will connect and regularly meet with a therapist and life coach to unpack my past, deal with my present and break the chains of bondage for my future posterity.

REFLECTIONS

_____

_____

_____

_____

_____

_____

_____

_____

_____

_____

_____

_____

_____

_____

_____

AFFIRMATION 18:

GREATER HUMILITY

"Don't be impressed with your own wisdom. Instead, fear The Lord and turn away from evil. Then you will have healing for your body and strength for your bones."
– Proverbs 3:7-8

No one likes a know it all. Don't get me wrong. You can know a lot of things and have vast experience in different arenas, but no one person knows IT ALL. I hate to break it to you, but unless you are Jesus Jr., somebody somewhere is smarter than you. In fact, let me start there. You didn't create yourself, so even YOU don't know everything about yourself. To bring health to your body and nourishment to your bones, start by developing a relationship with God and doing things that are pleasing to Him. Next, in the words of Rihanna, if you want to "shine bright like a diamond," you have to be willing to be cut like a diamond. Ask God to lead you to people that are more successful than you in marriage and in business. Learn from them and apply their instructions. If these are good "gemologists," they'll have you making adjustments that are uncomfortable to ensure you eventually sparkle brightly for all the world to see and admire.

Now please understand there's a difference between learning from them and trying to become them. What do I mean? If you ask someone for advice, say for marital advice, for example, that doesn't mean you have to do every single thing that person suggests. What works for one couple may absolutely not work for another. It's fine to hear someone out when he or she is dispensing advice, but don't think you have to implement every single suggestion in your life. Determine what works best for you and your spouse — or you and your boyfriend/girlfriend — and go from there. While success leaves clues, marriages and relationships aren't one size fits all. The same goes with financial advice, spiritual advice — or any kind of advice. Listen intently, unless it's clear the person is off his or her rocker, but then pray on it and do what works best for you.

Let me give you some free game here as well. While you're seeking mentorship, make sure you're being a mentor to someone else. If you're just trying to get value without giving value, you're doing it wrong. No one likes a taker. (The doors of the church are now open...is there one?)

#WinYourDay Affirmation:

Today, I will humble myself and seek to learn from people who are smarter and more accomplished than me—instead of being wise in my own eyes.

REFLECTIONS

_____

_____

_____

_____

_____

_____

_____

_____

_____

_____

_____

_____

_____

_____

_____

_____

_____

AFFIRMATION 19:

GREATER AWARENESS

*"So I run with purpose in every step.
I am not just shadowboxing."
– 1 Corinthians 9:26*

It's hard to hit a target you can't see. How do you know you need to lose twenty pounds if you haven't stepped on the scale because you're afraid of what it might say? If you truly want to win your health, first begin by taking inventory of where you are. How much do you weigh? How much do you want to weigh? What kinds of foods are you eating that helped you reach your current weight? What adjustments do you need to make to reach your ideal weight? Let me be the first to tell you, exercise without dietary adjustments is counterproductive. I'll explain tomorrow.

The key to winning your health (and every other area of your life for that matter,) is self-awareness. If you're overweight, what triggers you to eat or drink certain foods? If going to the gym consumes your life, why? If you become aware of not only where you are, but also of how you got there, it will exponentially increase your chances of success. Here's a simple but by no means easy formula for success: Identify your triggers. Make the adjustments. Win your life! See? Simple! Not easy, but simple.

#WinYourDay Affirmation:
Today, I will identify what got me to where I am, and I will make the decision to either do less or more of those things to achieve optimal health.

REFLECTIONS

_____

_____

_____

_____

_____

_____

_____

_____

_____

_____

_____

_____

_____

_____

_____

_____

_____

AFFIRMATION 20:

GREATER DISCIPLINE

"I discipline my body like an athlete, training it to do what it should. Otherwise, I fear that after preaching to others I myself might be disqualified."
– 1 Corinthians 9:27

I used to be a personal trainer at Bally Total Fitness. I knew how to train people to add muscle to their bodies; however, I didn't know how to help them get fat off. I'd help my clients bench three hundred fifteen pounds or more, but also say they could eat whatever they wanted because I'd work it off of them. LIES. They'd remark that their chest was swollen, but complain that their stomach was, too! Needless to say, I didn't have this job long. In my defense though, all they had to do was look at me. I mean, I was out here looking like E. Honda! What did they expect?! Shout out to all my Street Fighter peeps.

The reality is you're going to have to make changes in your diet AND exercise routines to be physically healthy. Come on fam?! Just put the fork down already. Turn the TV off and get some rest. SportsCenter shows the same sports highlights over and over, so why must you watch it over and over again? You mean to tell me you'd rather watch an athlete compete at his or her highest level, while earning crazy dollars, instead of competing at your highest level and living your blessed life? At some point, you're going to have to be disciplined and just tell yourself no.

Lastly, allow me to give you some advice that will tie yesterday's and today's scriptures together to highlight their fullest meaning.

1. Stop grinding with no purpose. Busy doesn't equal successful.

2. Stop telling other people what to do when you're not doing those things yourself.

#WinYourDay Affirmation:
Today, I will create and stick to a plan for my health goals; and, I will practice what I preach.

REFLECTIONS

_____

_____

_____

_____

_____

_____

_____

_____

_____

_____

_____

_____

_____

_____

_____

_____

_____

_____

AFFIRMATION 21:

GREATER WEIGHTLIFTING

"...let us strip off every weight that slows us down..."
– Hebrews 12:1

Weightlifting is crucial to your success! Sure, you could drop weight and be skinny, but most everyone desires to be toned with some semblance of muscle. No one gets sculpted arms without curling. No one gets amazing pecs without pressing. And please...don't skip leg day! But you know what's more important than lifting physical weight? Lifting spiritual weight. What's holding you down? What's holding you back? Is it lust? Gambling? Lying? Fellas, I know she's thick, but so is the anointing on your life. A few moments of pleasure aren't worth sacrificing your purpose. Ladies, I know he's fine and has been promising to marry you. Or, maybe you're feeling like Whitney Houston in "Waiting to Exhale" when she said, "My body needs this." But is the sex really worth jeopardizing your destiny? Seriously, how many more times are you going to say, "Lord, if you just get me out of this bed and back home safely I'll never fool around with him again?"

Do me a favor. As you're seeking physical health, be as persistent in your pursuit of spiritual health. One will help you look good on earth, but the other will ensure you look good in heaven. Most of us want to be in relationships, but instead of waiting for the "right person" to come along, sometimes it's best to remain single until we become the "right person." Remember, just as "Waiting to Exhale" was a popular movie, so was "I Can Do Bad By Myself."

As you're lifting weight, think of God as your spotter. The role of the spotter is to make sure you don't hurt yourself by trying to lift too much at once. Sadly, for whatever reason, I've seen spotters abandon the person lifting weights, often causing injuries. People may at times abandon you because of your spiritual weight, but God has promised to always be here for you. God is always on your side and will never abandon you. God is always willing to listen to your problems and to try to help you. God is the one who allowed His Son, Jesus, to die on the cross for your sins and mine so that we might have eternal life. (John 3:16.) "God is your ultimate spiritual spotter." If you find a man or woman on earth with whom to help you lift weights, then as the old folks say, "that's extra gravy." But God is who you need first and foremost. With Him, a lot of the other important things in your life just may come into place.

#WinYourDay Affirmation:
Today, I will lay aside every weight and the sin that clings so close to me, and will instead run with endurance the race that is set before me to be physically, spiritually, mentally, emotionally and financially healthy!

REFLECTIONS

WEEK FOUR
FINANCES

"The person who doesn't know where his next
dollar is coming from usually doesn't know
where his last dollar went."

- Unknown

AFFIRMATION 22:

GREATER GRIND

"Work brings profit, but mere talk leads to poverty!"
– Proverbs 14:23

Someone once coined the phrase, "Talk is cheap!" Earlier in this book, I mentioned the importance of speaking things into existence. However, speaking in and of itself won't produce the greater you're looking to achieve. Think of speaking your dreams as a means of priming the pump. As you speak, the universe responds by orchestrating that chance phone call, or that impromptu business meeting that will change everything. But in case no one has ever told you, it's your work that's going to prepare you for said phone call. It's your work that's going to prepare you for the meeting. Someone else once said, "Luck favors the prepared." Can you imagine going into a one hundred million-dollar business meeting unprepared? Sadly, many of you aren't prepared for your greater because your work ethic is trash. You have multimillion-dollar dreams but a work ethic that couldn't buy a $3 cup of coffee!

And not only do some of you need to check your work ethic; you need to check your resume. If you don't believe that sometimes it's your resume – what you and what others say about you – that keeps you from getting your foot in the door, believe it. Some hiring managers are so strict that if they see even one typo on a resume, or, if they hear or see one questionable thing on your social media profile, they immediately trash it without giving the would-be candidate a second thought. Make sure your resume is up-to-date and that it accurately and attractively states your experience. Make sure your resume sings and makes others want to bring you in for an interview — if not hire you outright. Make sure your resume reflects the professional that you are and is on point. If you want to succeed financially, just remember the five P's:

#WinYourDay Affirmation:

1. Pray — Pray for my financial success.
2. Proclaim — Declare that I am a multimillionaire or a billionaire with a B.
3. Plan — Plan my success strategy.
4. Produce — Get to work, and make sure my work-
   ethic speaks highly of who I am.
5. Profit — Secure the bag.

REFLECTIONS

_____

_____

_____

_____

_____

_____

_____

_____

_____

_____

_____

_____

_____

_____

_____

_____

_____

_____

AFFIRMATION 23:

GREATER FREEDOM

"Know the state of your flocks, and put your heart into caring for your herds"
- Proverbs 27:23

Sometimes our financial success isn't about making more money. It's about being faithful over what we already have. To be faithful over what we have, we must first know what we have! Sadly, many people don't operate on a budget. They get their checks and spend, spend, spend — yes, even on the bills — until the checks are completely gone. Most of us have lived paycheck to paycheck at some point in our lives. And let's not even mention how reckless we can be when it comes to credit card spending. We go to a store, see something we like, know we don't have the cash on hand or in the bank to purchase the item and reach into our wallets or purses for the card and charge it. Some of us do this throughout the year, but we really do it at Christmas when we feel obligated to give gifts to our friends and family members. We charge, charge, charge, all the while telling ourselves that we'll pay the card's balance off the next month. Then the bill comes and we're scratching our heads because we have no idea how a few gifts ended up costing a few grand. Now we're in debt up to our eyeballs and stressed about how we're going to pay the bill.

If you're not a good steward over the thirty thousand per year job, how will making one hundred thousand per year help? You'll just end up spending more because you have access to more. I've seen people who earn thirty thousand per year become debt free, take a family vacation every year and enjoy life to the fullest. I've also seen people who earn high six figures experience a layoff, shutdown or furlough for just one month and the next month have to move out of their mansions and into their cars. Remember, you must first be faithful over the few before you can be made ruler of many.

#WinYourDay Affirmation:
Today, I will identify all of my income, all of my debt and will create (and stick to) a plan to become completely debt free.

REFLECTIONS

_____

_____

_____

_____

_____

_____

_____

_____

_____

_____

_____

_____

_____

_____

_____

_____

AFFIRMATION 24:

GREATER SAVINGS

³⁴ Then Pharaoh should appoint supervisors over the land and let them collect one-fifth of all the crops during the seven good years. ³⁵ Have them gather all the food produced in the good years that are just ahead and bring it to Pharaoh's storehouses. Store it away, and guard it so there will be food in the cities. ³⁶ That way there will be enough to eat when the seven years of famine come to the land of Egypt. Otherwise this famine will destroy the land."
– Genesis 41:34-36

One of my favorite people in the Bible is Joseph, to whom God gave the ability to interpret dreams. God gave Pharaoh two different dreams that had the same meaning: Egypt and surrounding areas would experience seven years of plenty, then seven years of lack that would completely erase all memory of the plentiful years.

Joseph, operating in his God-given gift, advises Pharaoh to save most of the grain produced during the plentiful years so there wouldn't be any lack in Egypt. When the famine struck, the people of Egypt were able to rely on their savings. Not only was it enough for them during the seven years; they were able to save surrounding nations from starvation as well.

What if Egypt had disregarded Joseph's advice and decided to live it up during their plentiful years? Their disobedience would have not only resulted in their deaths, but also in the deaths of people in other countries. The world tells us every day to live it up and enjoy life to the fullest because YOLO — You Only Live Once. This is faulty reasoning, and following the world's advice could cause you irreparable harm.

Need further proof that you need to save? The COVID-19 global pandemic pretty much ravished the world overnight for goodness sakes. Most people who lost their income sources didn't have enough money saved, so they were stuck at home quarantining with very little money with which to buy food and pay bills. That alone should make it clear that having money set aside for a rainy day—or a whole year like 2020 for that matter—is a necessity.

#WinYourDay Affirmation:

Today, I will show God that I am a good steward of what He's blessed me with by saving money from all of my sources of income.

REFLECTIONS

_____

_____

_____

_____

_____

_____

_____

_____

_____

_____

_____

_____

_____

_____

_____

_____

_____

AFFIRMATION 25:

GREATER INVESTING

*"But divide your investments among many places,
for you do not know what risks might lie ahead."
– Ecclesiastes 11:2*

Don't believe the hype: Your job, no matter how good
you are at it, how much you love it or how much it pays,
will never be enough to make you wealthy. You should
always have multiple streams of income. However, those
who are truly successful have a baseline job. Here's the
point most people miss concerning streams. A stream
forms from a high point on earth and runs down to lower
points. If everything works perfectly, all of the different
streams meet and form a river or other larger body of
water. Geologists, don't crucify me, as I realize this is just
a rough definition.

My point is we all need to work. However, the key to success is to never put all of your hope into one job or career. One aspect to financial greater is to use your job to
create other income sources. For example, you could
make and monetize YouTube videos. Or, you could create and sell products online. You could even invest in
the stock market. (If you invest, do your homework and
don't just put money into stocks that "look good" or

"sound promising." Remember, just as easily as you can make money in the stock market; you can lose it.) What I'm trying to say is, let your job fund your businesses, and let your businesses fund your future. In this country, many if not all states operate under what's called at-will employment, meaning an employer can let you go without cause. Never put your family's future in the hands of one organization.

#WinYourDay Affirmation:

Today, I will determine what gifts I have that will create other streams of income. And if I don't have a job, I will get one!

REFLECTIONS

_____

_____

_____

_____

_____

_____

_____

_____

_____

_____

_____

_____

_____

_____

_____

_____

AFFIRMATION 26:

GREATER GIVING

7 You must each decide in your heart how much to give.
And don't give reluctantly or in response to pressure.
"For God loves a person who gives cheerfully." 8 And God
will generously provide all you need. Then you will always
have everything you need and plenty left
over to share with others.
– 2 Corinthians 9:7-8

Our world teaches us to get all we can. Then, after we've gotten all we can, get some more. It's funny how we believe the more stuff we have the happier we'll be. However, God tells us that the more we give away— not the more we keep—the happier we become. Better yet, the more blessed we become. For us to win in our finances, we need to remember three giving principles:

1. We should give regularly. In 1 Corinthians 16:2, the believers were instructed to put aside their offerings each week. My wife and I personally put aside our tithes and offerings each time we get paid. Whether weekly, bi-weekly, bi-monthly or monthly, we should all give regularly and not just one time to pat our- selves on the back. If we give regularly, we will be blessed regularly.

2. We should give according to what we have. In that same verse, the believers were to set aside a portion of the money they'd earned. The system my wife and I follow is to give ten percent of our earnings for tithes then an additional offering between five and ten percent. Remember, the amount given won't be equal for everyone, but the principle remains the same. Now I'm not saying you have to give like we do, but success leaves clues.

3. We should give cheerfully. 2 Corinthians 9:6-7 says, "...Whoever sows sparingly will also reap sparingly, and whoever sows bountifully will also reap bountifully. Each one must give as he has decided in his heart, not reluctantly or under compulsion, for God loves a cheerful giver." It's a great thing when we give our money to our local church or charity. But don't let any pastor or organization manipulate you into giving. Also, if we were to follow the principles in these few verses, God says He will generously give to us—so much so that not only will all of our needs be taken care of but we'll be able to give and share with others! Crazy huh? If we give cheerfully, God will give back to us so we can start the process all over again. We'd be silly not to follow this financial success formula.

#WinYourDay Affirmation:
Today, I will create a plan to give according to my income. I will give regularly and cheerfully.

REFLECTIONS

_____

_____

_____

_____

_____

_____

_____

_____

_____

_____

_____

_____

_____

_____

_____

_____

_____

AFFIRMATION 27:

GREATER CONTENTMENT

[11] Not that I was ever in need, for I have learned how to be content with whatever I have. [12] I know how to live on almost nothing or with everything. I have learned the secret of living in every situation, whether it is with a full stomach or empty, with plenty or little.
- Philippians 4:11-12

Your coworker just came back from a ten-day vacation on some exotic island. Your neighbors just bought a luxury car or soon will no longer be your neighbors because they just closed on a mansion in a ritzy part of town. Your friend's husband was able to buy her that exclusive handbag for which people have been on a waitlist for years. People like to refer to this phenomenon as pocket watching.

Sometimes we end up seeing the blessings of others and wanting the same things for ourselves. Or worse, we end up going into debt trying to obtain what they have just so we can "belong," which is more commonly referred to as keeping up with the Joneses. There's nothing inherently wrong with desiring the blessings of others. If I see my friend move into his dream house, it should motivate me to want to move into my dream house too! However, we should always be content with the blessings we currently have. Being content doesn't mean we can't desire more. It just means that we are satisfied with what we have until more comes.

A scripture that gets at this in a different way, if you will, is one that's oft-quoted: Jeremiah 29:11 — "For I know the plans I have for you declares The Lord. Plans to prosper you and not to harm you. Plans to give you hope and a future." Now, even though I said a few sentences ago that there's nothing inherently wrong with desiring the blessings of others, please know that God already has a plan for you. And just think, He had it even before you were born. That's right. Before you were born. Moving into a ritzy neighborhood might be good for your neighbors, but you could get there and find that the people are "too stuck up" or there are so many rules in the subdivision that you feel as though you can no longer truly enjoy your home and have fun there. Your friend might have an exclusive handbag, but would you rather have an exclusive handbag and no money in it or a much less expensive handbag and the $2,500 that it cost in the bank? Learn to be content with what you have. After all, what you have just might be what you truly need.

#WinYourDay Affirmation:
Today, I will take note of all of my blessings and be grateful for each one.

REFLECTIONS

_____

_____

_____

_____

_____

_____

_____

_____

_____

_____

_____

_____

_____

_____

_____

_____

_____

_____

AFFIRMATION 28:

GREATER PRIORITIES

"Seek the Kingdom of God above all else, and live
righteously, and He will give you everything you need."
– Matthew 6:33

It's amazing the number of the things we stress about on a daily basis. How am I going to pay my bills? Why am I still single? Why is the marriage I prayed for struggling to survive? I've worked out for a week. Why don't I have a six pack yet? As we close this week, allow me to give you the ultimate formula for financial success.

First, truly seek God. Don't seek Him just when you want something. Don't seek Him just when you have a pressing need. Seek Him at all times. Prayer, fasting, Bible study and engaging with other like-minded believers are all excellent ways to seek The Lord. Seek Him like you seek that best vacation price. Seek Him like you seek likes on the Gram.

Second, not only should you seek God; you should seek His righteousness. Not what you think is righteous; what He says is righteous. Being a good husband or wife is righteous. Being a good father or mother is righteous.

Becoming the best version of yourself, with the help of the Holy Ghost, is righteous. At the end of the day, don't let it be said that you secured the bag but lost your family, reputation, or worse your soul.

And let me give you some more free game: Don't seek a come up so bad that you're willing to compromise your character for it. Too many people seek elevation, but when they rise their characters aren't able to sustain the altitude. And now that they've fallen, they're in a worse position than before because their credibility is damaged. Don't let this be you. Character and integrity matter.

When you seek Him first, and His righteousness, all of the things that we need (even some of the things that we want) get added to our lives.

#WinYourDay Affirmation:
Today, I will seek the Lord and His righteousness with every fiber of my being.

REFLECTIONS

BONUS: DAYS 29 & 30

FUN

Always work hard and have fun in what you do because I think that's when you're more successful. You have to choose to do it.

- Simone Biles

AFFIRMATION 29:

GREATER FUN // PART 1

So I decided there is nothing better than to enjoy food and drink and to find satisfaction in work. Then I realized that these pleasures are from the hand of God.
– Ecclesiastes 2:24

Who doesn't like taking exotic vacations? Who doesn't like going on a date to a nice restaurant and not worrying about how the bill will be paid? Who wouldn't want to live in a nice, big home and drive a luxury car? There is absolutely nothing wrong with liking, desiring and even experiencing nice things! The text today says that all of these come from God. Don't listen to people who tell you that wanting nice things makes you materialistic. If I obediently seek God first and His righteousness, and then He adds everything unto me in return like He promised, I'm going to enjoy everything He has for me and I'm going to do it in the biggest way possible. Sorry not sorry.

Of course, the key is to always remember to thank and praise God for the ways in which He blesses you. Likewise, never think you're better than anyone else just because you might live in a bigger, more expensive house, drive a fancier car, have a higher salary or live in a better part of town. None of us is better than anyone else. God created ALL OF US in His image. If you are blessed with some of the finer things in life, don't get the big head over it. Also, remember that some of the most unhappy people on the planet are those who seemingly "have it all."

#WinYourDay Affirmation:

Today, I will stop allowing broke pocket-watchers to make me feel guilty because I've sought God, worked hard and am now enjoying the rewards of my labor.

REFLECTIONS

_____

_____

_____

_____

_____

_____

_____

_____

_____

_____

_____

_____

_____

_____

_____

_____

AFFIRMATION 30:

GREATER FUN // PART 2

[19] And it is a good thing to receive wealth from God and the good health to enjoy it. To enjoy your work and accept your lot in life—this is indeed a gift from God. [20] God keeps such people so busy enjoying life that they take no time to brood over the past.
- Ecclesiastes 5:19-20

Before I fully gave my life to Christ, my idea of having fun was going to the club every Saturday. My friends and I would open the club at ten and close it down at four in the morning. And if we wanted to take our so-called fun to another level, after we left that club at four in the morning, we'd go to the only club that stayed open until seven (Club 112...if you know, you know.) Yes, fun for me at that time in my life was full of debauchery.

When I fully gave my life to Christ, I knew I could not engage in those things anymore. The problem was, I still wanted to have fun but no one at the church could show me how to have fun as a Christian. You see, sometimes the church has a habit of telling us everything we can't do, as opposed to telling us the things we can do. Simply put, having fun as a Christian means doing things that will bring a smile to your face and also to God's face. In all actuality, I see having fun as a Christian as the greatest evangelistic tool ever. When people see a smile on my face, joy in my heart and me enjoying life to the fullest, they are instinctively going to ask me how I'm able to do those things. And my response should be that because I have delighted myself in God, He has given me the desires of my heart.

To name a few things, now fun for me is spending time with God in prayer. Now fun for me is making sure my body, mind and soul are all in a place of optimal health. Now fun for me is being able to tell my wife we're flying first class to a romantic beach bungalow and she doesn't need to pack because we'll shop for the items we need when we get there. Now fun for me is being able to leave an inheritance to my children's children. And now fun for me is honoring God by using all of my gifts, skills, talents and abilities to add value to everyone I come in contact with, which ultimately shows them how to have an awesome relationship with God and possibly leads them to experience some fun of their own.

Simply put, fun isn't stressing about how I'm going to make ends meet. Fun is enjoying my relationship with God, being who He's called me to be, doing what He's called me to do and enjoying all of the blessings He has bestowed upon me.

#WinYourDay Affirmation:

Today, I will find my God and find my fun.

REFLECTIONS

_____

_____

_____

_____

_____

_____

_____

_____

_____

_____

_____

_____

_____

_____

_____

_____

CONCLUSION

It is my prayer that our journey over these last thirty days has blessed you tremendously. I also pray that you found some inspiration and strategies in this book that will change your life for the better. At the end of the day, if your life, or at least your outlook on life, is the same as it was thirty days ago, then you really need to ask yourself what can you do to change YOU. Remember, the promises of God are not actual; they are optional. You can claim them all you want, but until you actually put in the work to change your faith, family, fitness, finances and fun, you'll never get to the places God wants to take you in life.

On a transparent note, I'm still on my journey to achieve greater. While I've had successes in implementing the strategies in this book, I'm not where I want to be. Yet, I praise God I'm not where I used to be either. True greater is seeking to become the person God has created you to be every single day of your life. As you become better in the areas of your faith, family, fitness, finances and fun, celebrate your victories along the way — just don't settle for them. Each day, strive to become better than you were yesterday because as long as you're alive the journey never stops. There's always new levels to unlock.

Also, while you're on your journey to greater, make sure you help someone else along the way to get to at least where you've gotten. In the words of Mahalia Jackson, "If I can help somebody as I pass along, then my living shall not be in vain."

So, do me a huge favor if you haven't already: Beginning today, decide every day you awaken to become a better person than you were the day before. Decide to become closer to God and put in the work to make it happen. Decide to be a better husband or wife, son or daughter, father, mother or legal guardian — and put in the work to make it happen. Decide on being healthier physically, mentally and emotionally — and put in the work to make it happen. Decide to identify and cultivate your gift(s), enabling them to make room for you. And decide on having more fun and enjoying your life — and put in the work to make it happen. I can't wait to see how the new version of you changes the world.

Always remember, you are
#CalledToSomethingGreater

Darrell A. Palmes, III

To Robyn, Brittany and Alonzo—I Love You.

BOOK DARRELL
TODAY

Want to book Darrell to speak at your next virtual or in person event? Please contact him at 404.259.1774.

NEED A
COACH?

Purchasing this book was just the beginning, as there's only so much you can do by yourself! Everyone needs help getting to the next level, and Darrell is expertly qualified to help you in your quest to achieve greater in your life and in your relationships.

Visit www.darrellpalmes.org/coaching and schedule your coaching session today.

CONNECT WITH
DARRELL

FOLLOW DARRELL ON SOCIAL MEDIA!
Instagram/Facebook/Twitter | @darrellpalmes

Made in the USA
Columbia, SC
02 December 2021

50241252R00069